Water Wise

THE WATER CYCLE

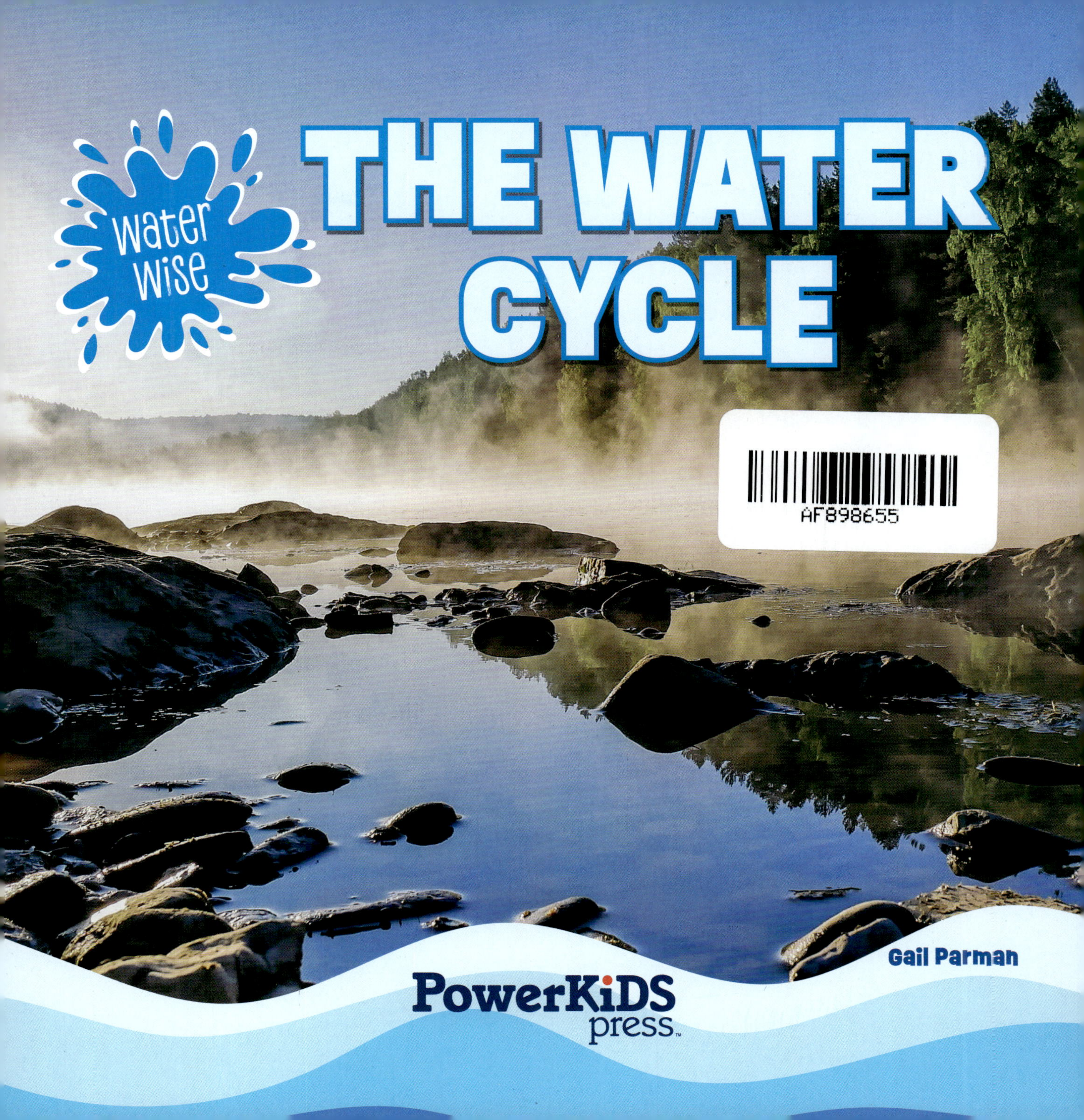

Gail Parman

PowerKiDS press

Published in 2027 by
The Rosen Publishing Group, Inc.
2544 Clinton Street, Buffalo, NY 14224

Designer: Beeline Media and Design
Editor: Tricia Hoffman

Portions of this work were originally authored by Barbara M. Linde and published as W*here's the Water?: The Water Cycle*. All new material in this edition is authored by Gail Parman.

Photo credits: Cover, p. 1 sanbeliaev/Shutterstock.com; cover, p. 1 SaltyArts Design/Shutterstock.com; cover, p. 1, 4, 6, 8, 10, 12, 14, 16, 18, 20, 21, 24 (wave) vectorstuff/Shutterstock.com; p. 4 PhotoJuli86/Shutterstock.com; p. 5 TinnaPong/Shutterstock.com; p. 7 p.tapenko/Shutterstock.com; p. 9 buradaki/Shutterstock.com; p. 10 Delpixel/Shutterstock.com; p. 11 Cacio Murilo/Shutterstock.com; p. 12 New Africa/Shutterstock.com; p. 13 KrimKate/Shutterstock.com; p. 14 b113/Shutterstock.com; p. 15 Michal Balada/Shutterstock.com; p. 17 AustralianCamera/Shutterstock.com; p. 18 Maiquel Jantsch/Shutterstock.com; p. 19 HusnainPhotographer/Shutterstock.com; p. 21 Platon Anton/Shutterstock.com

Cataloging-in-Publication Data
Names: Parman, Gail.
Title: The water cycle / Gail Parman.
Description: Buffalo, New York : PowerKids Press, 2027. | Series: Water wise | Includes glossary and index.
Identifiers: ISBN 9781499458343 (pbk.) | ISBN 9781499458350 (library bound) | ISBN 9781499458367 (ebook)
Subjects: LCSH: Hydrologic cycle--Juvenile literature.
Classification: LCC GB848.P377 2027 | DDC 551.48 --dc23

Printed in China

CPSIA Compliance Information: Batch #QSPK27. For Further Information contact Rosen Publishing at 1-800-237-9932.

Contents

Water Is Everywhere!

Think of all the places on Earth you might find water. There's some in a **puddle** on the sidewalk. There's more in lakes, rivers, and small streams. A lot of water is in the ocean. You've seen rain falling from the sky. Perhaps you've even played in snow or seen hailstones.

Where does this water come from? And where does it go if it dries up? You'll learn the answers to these questions and more as you read all about the water cycle.

Go with the Flow

The water cycle is the continuous movement of water on, above, and below Earth's surface. A cycle is a set of events that happen the same way over and over again.

Water is a big part of our lives. We drink it every day. We use it to wash, cook, and even to flush the toilet!

Earth's Water

For a long time, many scientists had a **theory** that Earth's water came from **meteorites** and **comets** hitting the planet after it formed. But now, some scientists think that Earth may have had the **ingredients** to make water from the beginning.

In 2025, a team of scientists studied very old meteorites. The meteorites were found to have a makeup like that of the oldest rocks on Earth. The meteorites also contained hydrogen, which is an important ingredient for water. This made the scientists think that Earth might have formed with everything it needed to make water.

Go with the Flow
Water is made up of hydrogen and oxygen.

Water is everywhere, but how did it get here in the first place? No one knows for sure, but scientists are getting closer to finding the answer.

A Watery World

Water covers more than 70 percent of Earth's surface. It exists in three forms—liquid, solid, and gas. It's in liquid form in bodies of water such as oceans, lakes, rivers, and streams. Some liquid water flows underground too. This is called groundwater.

When water is frozen, it becomes a solid. Snow, glaciers, and ice caps are all types of solid water. Some water exists as a gas called water vapor. You can't see it, but you may be able to feel it on a very humid day!

Go with the Flow

Most of Earth's water is salt water in the oceans. Only about 1 percent of the water on Earth is fresh water that people can drink.

Earth is mostly water. When seen from space, it looks much more like a blue planet than a green one!

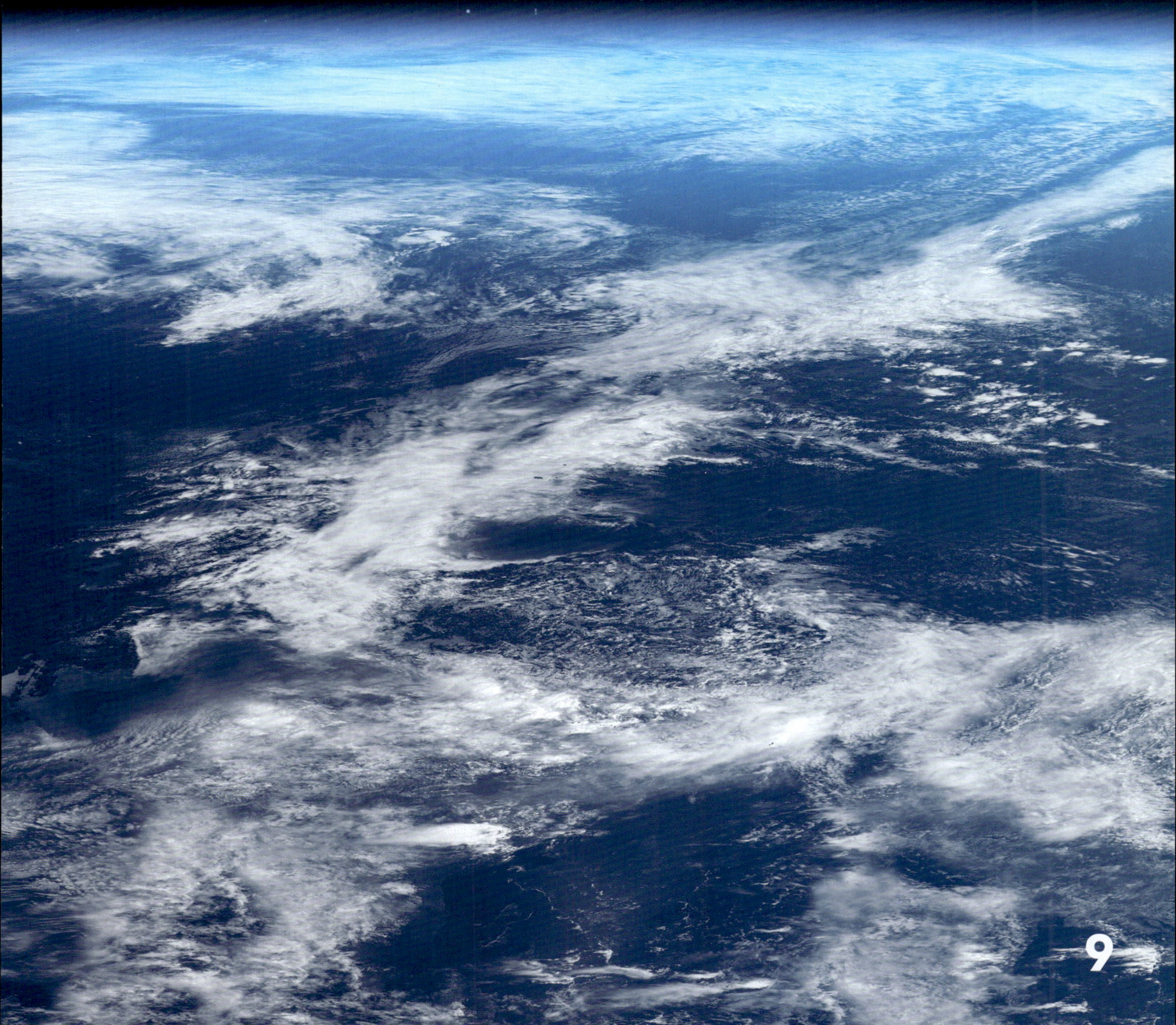

The Cycle Continues

Planet Earth has a set amount of water. Very little is ever added or lost. The same water has been moving around on the ground, underground, and in the sky for billions of years. In fact, it's been moving around the planet since Earth formed! This continuous movement is called the water cycle.

There are three main parts of the water cycle: evaporation, condensation, and **precipitation**. The water cycle never stops!

Go with the Flow

The water cycle connects all water on Earth. It also affects the weather and climate.

Because it's a cycle, there's no set beginning or end to water's movement. It is continuously recycled.

From Liquid to Gas

Evaporation is an important part of the water cycle. It happens when water **molecules** warm up and change from a liquid to a gas. This gas, or water vapor, rises into the air. After it evaporates, a water molecule stays in the **atmosphere** for about 10 days before returning to Earth.

Most evaporation takes place over oceans because they're the largest bodies of water. Water also evaporates from lakes, rivers, and wet ground. Ice can melt into liquid water and then evaporate. Sometimes, ice evaporates without melting first. When this happens, it is called sublimation.

Go with the Flow

When water evaporates from a plant's leaves, it is called **transpiration**.

Heat causes water to change from liquid to gas. When you're boiling water on the stove, you may see water vapor rising as steam. Evaporation can also happen more slowly at lower temperatures, like when puddles dry up on a warm day.

From Gas to Liquid

After water evaporates, the water vapor rises into the air. The higher it gets, the colder the air becomes. The colder air cools the water vapor and changes it back into tiny liquid water droplets. The change of water from a gas to a liquid is called condensation.

Water droplets clump together to form a cloud. The droplets keep getting cooler. The cloud grows larger as more droplets join the others. When a cloud gets too heavy, it may begin to rain or snow—and the next part of the water cycle begins.

Go with the Flow

Clouds might look light and fluffy, but they can be really heavy. A cloud can weigh as much as a jet!

Condensation doesn't just happen high up in the atmosphere. Fog is condensation that forms close to Earth's surface.

Coming Back Down

Water in the clouds comes back to Earth as precipitation. When the temperature is warm, precipitation falls as rain. When it's cold, precipitation falls as snow. But precipitation can take on other forms as well.

Sleet is rain that freezes into tiny pellets as it falls. It hits the ground as icy slush. Freezing rain falls as liquid but freezes to a solid when it reaches the ground. It can make the ground quite slippery. Hailstones are balls of ice that may fall during a thunderstorm—sometimes even in the summer!

Go with the Flow

Rain doesn't always make the ground wet! In very dry or very hot places, rain can evaporate before it hits the ground.

When the temperature drops to 32 degrees Fahrenheit (0 degrees Celsius) or below, precipitation can fall as snow. But most precipitation falls as rain.

Water Storage

Some of Earth's water is always part of the cycle of evaporation, condensation, and precipitation. The rest is stored. It stays in the same form for a long time. For example, a lot of water exists as ice in Antarctica and Greenland.

Some water is stored underground after it soaks into soil during rainstorms or after snow melts. This is called groundwater, and people often dig wells to get to it. This water can be used as drinking water or for watering crops.

Go with the Flow
About 90 percent of the ice on Earth is in Antarctica.

Sometimes, big pieces of ice called icebergs break away. When they reach warm water, they melt.

Test It Out

On a warm day, try this experiment to watch evaporation in action! In the morning, go outside and pour the same amount of water into two clear plastic bowls. With a dry erase marker or piece of tape, mark a line to show where the water level begins. Set one bowl in the sun and one in the shade. Check them every hour or two. Mark the water level each time it changes.

What happens? At the end of the day, the water level of the bowl in the sun will likely be lower than the one in the shade. That's because the heat of the sun makes water evaporate faster!

Go with the Flow

Ask a grownup for help before starting this experiment.

The Water Cycle

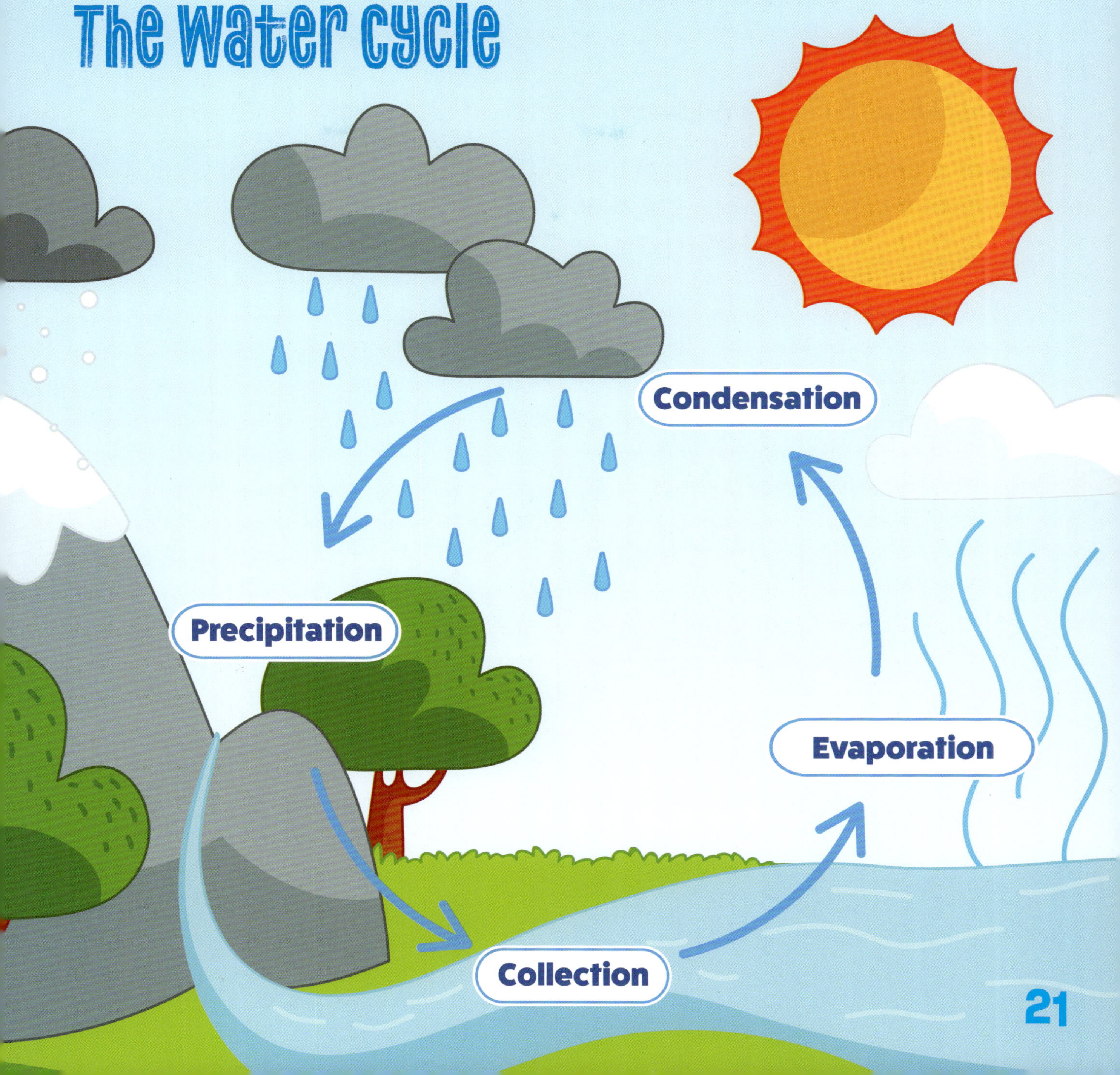

Glossary

atmosphere: the mix of gases that are all around Earth

comet: a space object made of ice and dust that has a long glowing tail when it passes close to the sun

ingredient: an item used to make something

meteorite: a piece of rock that falls to Earth from space

molecule: the smallest part of something

precipitation: rain, snow, sleet, or hail

puddle: a small pool of water

theory: an explanation based on facts that is generally accepted by scientists

transpiration: the giving off of water vapor through the leaves of plants

Fact Check

1. Water in a glacier is a __________.
   a. solid
   b. liquid
   c. gas

2. ________ happens when water molecules warm up and change from a liquid to a gas.
   a. evaporation
   b. condensation
   c. precipitation

3. Water condenses to form a cloud before coming back to Earth as ________.
   a. evaporation
   b. condensation
   c. precipitation

Answers: 1. a, 2. a, 3. c

On the Internet

Precipitation Education: The Water Cycle
pmm.nasa.gov/education/water-cycle
Read articles and watch videos to learn more about the water cycle.

Interactive Water Cycle Diagram for Kids
water.usgs.gov/edu/watercycle-kids-adv.html
Use this interactive website to take a virtual trip through the water cycle.

Publisher's note to educators and parents: Our editors have carefully reviewed these websites to ensure that they are suitable for students. Many websites change frequently, however, and we cannot guarantee that a site's future contents will continue to meet our high standards of quality and educational value. Be advised that students should be closely supervised whenever they access the Internet.

Index